MARTIAL ARTS

JUDO

Barnaby Chesterman (first dan black belt) is the official journalist of the International Judo Federation. Bob Willingham (fourth dan black belt) is the official photographer of the International Judo Federation. The models are Miles Goodman (junior orange belt), Carlos Thomas (junior yellow belt), Jenny Richards (junior green belt), Jene-Rene Badrick (junior brown belt), Colleen Kerr (junior brown belt), Robin Willingham (junior white belt), and Josh Shorlands (junior yellow belt).

Special thanks to Norman Miller of Judo, Inc. for fact-checking assistance.

Please visit our web site at: **www.garethstevens.com**
For a free color catalog describing Gareth Stevens Publishing's
list of high-quality books and multimedia programs,
call 1-800-542-2595 (USA) or 1-800-387-3178 (Canada).
Gareth Stevens Publishing's fax: (414) 332-3567.

Library of Congress Cataloging-in-Publication Data

Chesterman, Barnaby.
    Judo / Barnaby Chesterman, Bob Willingham. — North American ed.
       p. cm. — (Martial arts)
    Includes bibliographical references and index.
    ISBN 0-8368-4192-1 (lib. bdg.)
    1. Judo—Juvenile literature. I. Willingham, Bob. II. Title. III. Martial arts
(Milwaukee, Wis.)
  GV1114.C493   2004
  796.815'2—dc22   2004045208

This North American edition first published in 2005 by
Gareth Stevens Publishing
A World Almanac Education Group Company
330 West Olive Street, Suite 100
Milwaukee, WI 53212 USA

Original edition © 2003 by David West Children's Books. First published in Great Britain
in 2003 by Raintree, Halley Court, Jordan Hill, Oxford OX2 8EJ, part of Harcourt Education.
Raintree is a registered trademark of Harcourt Education Ltd. This U.S. edition © 2005 by
Gareth Stevens, Inc. Additional end matter © 2005 by Gareth Stevens, Inc.

Photographer: Bob Willingham
David West editor: James Pickering
David West designer: Gary Jeffrey
Gareth Stevens editor: Alan Wachtel
Gareth Stevens designer: Steve Schraenkler
Gareth Stevens art direction: Tammy West
Gareth Stevens production: Jessica Morris

Photo Credits:
Abbreviations: (t) top, (m) middle, (b) bottom, (r) right, (l) left, (c) center

Courtesy of Bob Willingham: cover, 6(all), 9(l), 9(b), 16(b), 21(tl), 24(tr), 27(tr), 27(mr), 29(all), 30(all).

Printed in the United States of America

1 2 3 4 5 6 7 8 9 08 07 06 05 04

MARTIAL ARTS

JUDO

Barnaby Chesterman
Bob Willingham

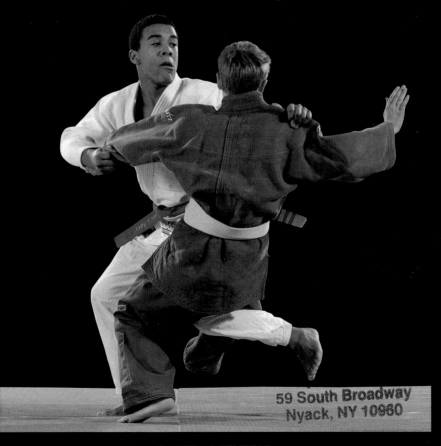

GARETH**STEVENS**
GS
PUBLISHING
A World Almanac Education Group Company

CONTENTS

INTRODUCTION

Martial arts are ways of learning to defend yourself and develop physical and mental discipline. Many of them are also international competitive sports. Experts agree that the only way to really learn a martial art is to train with a qualified teacher.

This book introduces some of the basic techniques of judo, a popular martial art that is also an Olympic sport. Read the text carefully and look closely at the pictures to see how to do some judo moves.

HISTORY

The origins of judo, or "the gentle way," lie in the ancient Japanese martial art of ju-jitsu, or "the compliant way," a form of open-hand, close-range combat that developed on medieval battlefields. The founder of judo was Jigoro Kano, a student of several forms of ju-jitsu.

Born in a Japanese village in 1860, Kano adapted some of the techniques of ju-jitsu into a sport and a form of self-defense.

Jigoro Kano was the founder of judo.

Yukio Tani was known as the "pocket Hercules."

Kano's main idea was to use minimal effort with maximum efficiency. He demonstrated his new martial-art style in competitions all over the world. One of Kano's top students, Yukio Tani, became famous for defeating men who were much bigger and stronger than he was.

In 1964, judo became an official Olympic sport. Anton Geesink, of the Netherlands, was the first Olympic gold medalist in judo.

Although Anton Geesink (right) had won the world championship in judo three years earlier, the Japanese were expected to win the Olympic gold medal in 1964.

CLOTHING AND ETIQUETTE

Judo is steeped in tradition. Even though it has developed into a modern martial art and sport, it still retains many of its original customs. Examples of judo customs are seen in the traditional clothing and etiquette that are still used.

The judo uniform (judogi) consists of loose pants and a thick jacket, closed by a belt (obi) that is passed twice around the waist and tied at the front.

RANKING SYSTEM

- white
- yellow
- orange
- green
- blue
- purple
- brown
- black

Judo uses a system of belt rankings to mark the accomplishments of more experienced participants from those of novices. A white belt is the lowest ranking and black is the highest. Brown and black belts usually are not awarded to anyone under the age of fifteen.

BOWING AND ETIQUETTE

Judo students bow (*rei*) to show respect for the martial art, for instructors, and for fellow students. In some schools, bows are performed when entering and leaving a judo hall (*dojo*), when stepping on and off the judo mat (*tatami*), and before and after any practice or demonstration. Judo etiquette also requires that students have clean bodies, clean uniforms, and high levels of personal sportsmanship.

JUDO ELEMENTS

Judo has four main elements that all students learn — throws, hold downs, armlocks, and chokes. Competitors must be above a minimum age to use armlocks and chokes in matches.

THROWS *(nage-waza)*

Throws are the most spectacular and dynamic element in judo. Judo uses four main types of throws — hand techniques (*te-waza*), foot sweeps (*ashi-waza*), hip throws (*koshi-waza*), and sacrifice throws (*sutemi-waza*). Whichever techniques a fighter prefers, the goal is always the same — to throw an opponent flat on the back with speed, power, and control.

HOLD DOWNS *(osaekomi-waza)*

When fighting on the ground, a judo competitor strives to control an opponent's shoulders and hold them to the mat. Holding an opponent to the mat for twenty-five seconds is called a hold down. A successful hold down wins a match.

ARMLOCKS *(kansetsu-waza)*

Armlocks are one type of submission technique. By putting pressure against an opponent's elbow joint, a competitor can force an opponent to give up. A fighter signals submission with two or more taps.

CHOKES *(shime-waza)*

The other type of submission technique in judo is the choke. Chokes put pressure against the side of an opponent's neck, cutting off blood circulation, or across an opponents throat, preventing him or her from breathing.

RULES

Judo competitions have many rules. A central referee and two corner judges enforce these rules.

Judo referees use a variety of arm motions to indicate the points they award and the decisions they make.

PROHIBITED ACTS

Various moves or actions are forbidden in judo, and they are punishable with penalties or disqualification.

Negative judo is a move in which a fighter tries to hold an opponent to prevent an attack. In judo, you must attack your opponent.

Holding one side of an opponent's jacket with both hands without attacking is not allowed for more than three seconds.

The pistol grip is banned because it is dangerous. Twisting the hand while holding with a pistol grip can damage an opponent's wrist.

Some dangerous offenses, such as pushing your opponent's face or striking out in any way, result in immediate disqualification.

SCORING

There are four ways to score in a judo competition, each of which has a penalty equivalent.

ippon: This score indicates an immediate victory. An *ippon* ends a judo match.

waza-ari: This is a half-point score. Two *waza-ari* equal one *ippon*.

yuko: This is a minor score. Any number of yuko add up to less than one *waza-ari*.

koka: This the lowest type of score. Any number of *koka* will always add up to less than one *yuko*.

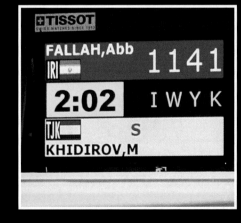

This is a judo scoreboard.

BREAKFALLS
(ukemi)

In judo, learning to fall without getting hurt is vital. Judo students practice four types of breakfalls: side, front, back, and rolling.

SIDE
From a crouching position, straighten one leg and topple to that side. Slap the mat with the arm straight and with fingers and toes pointing in the same direction.

FRONT
Crouch down with the feet together. Throw the arms forward and kick the legs back. Land on the forearms and toes, holding the rest of the body off the mat.

ROLLING
Step forward with the left leg, and put the right forearm on the mat in front of you. Roll over on the right shoulder and slap the mat with the left arm while landing. Also practice landing on the left side.

BACK
Use the back breakfall when an opponent throws you directly backward. Starting in a crouching position, kick the feet out to the front while falling backward. Slap the mat with both forearms and palms while landing.

EVASIONS

Judo students learn how to avoid, block, and twist away from opponent's attempts to throw them. In the text describing the pictures in this book, the person wearing blue is called "blue," and the person wearing white is called "white."

Cartwheels are good practice for avoiding landing on your back. It's always best to keep your back off the mat!

BREAKING THE GRIP

As white turns in to attack, blue pushes her hips into his backside. Blue then pulls her arm free from his grip as she turns her body away and steps backward.

BLOCKING

This is a good exercise to counter hip throws. When blue attacks with a hip throw, white drops his hips and spreads and bends his knees while wrapping his arms around blue's waist. White then pushes up with his hips and legs, lifting blue off the mat.

TWISTING

Being able to twist out of a throw and land on one's front is crucial. To show how to practice twisting out of a throw, white has blue hold his jacket as he leans backward, keeping his legs straight. When blue can no longer hold him and lets go, white quickly twists onto his front as he falls.

JUDO GAMES

It's important to have fun while learning judo. Not only are judo games fun, but they also teach important skills. Judo games can help improve strength, stamina, and mobility while encouraging a competitive spirit.

TUG OF WAR

This simple game builds leg strength. Blue and white tie a belt between their own belts, crouch down, and start crawling away from each other.

MONKEY RUNS

In this game, blue and white each take turns crawling across the mat with the other hanging on beneath. To trade positions, they don't let go of each other — they just roll over.

MOBILITY JUMP

This game is a test of explosiveness.

1. Three players line up, close together, ready to spring into action.

2. The boy in blue jumps left as the girl in white slides into the middle.

3. As she jumps right, the boy

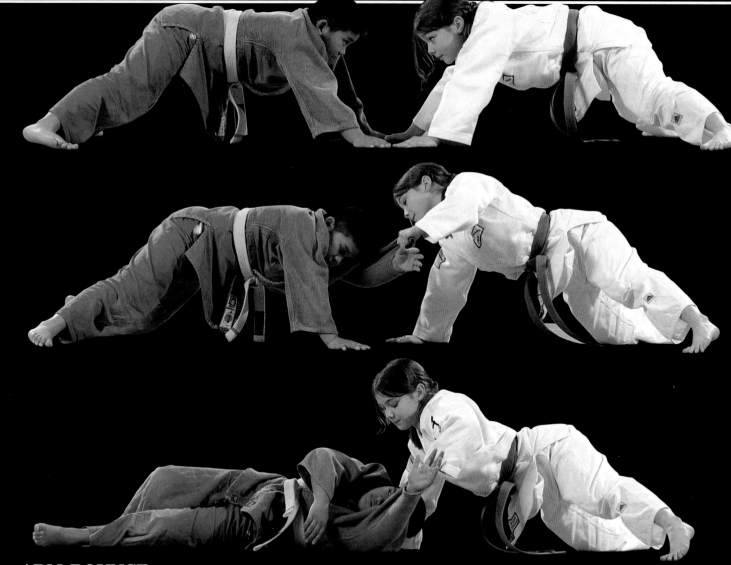

ARM BOUNCE

The arm bounce helps develop balance and the ability to attack and defend at the same time. Blue and white face each other while holding themselves up on their hands and feet with their arms and legs spread out for balance. Supporting themselves on one arm at a time, each tries to throw the other off balance by tapping or pulling the other's arm.

in white slides to the center.

4. The boy in white jumps to his left to complete the sequence.

5. All three get ready to continue the game — nonstop.

TRAINING

Judo students need to become physically fit and develop good technique. Judo is physically demanding, so students must be tough. Good technique is important because, no matter how strong you are, an opponent with good timing and speed will be able to throw you off balance.

Judo students practice grip fighting (kumi-kata) *to learn how to gain control of an opponent.*

CRASH MAT RUNNING
Practice running on a crash mat, keeping the knees up and pumping the arms. This is a very tiring exercise, but it builds strength and stamina in the legs. Many judo moves are made with the legs, so they must be in good condition.

FLOOR EXERCISES
1. Fast squat-thrusts are good for your legs.
2. Jumping jacks are good for all-around fitness and explosiveness. Jump as high as you can.

3. Sit-ups build the stomach muscles. Do them slowly to make them more effective.
4. Push-ups work the arms, shoulders, and chest. Touch your chest to the mat during each repetition.

TECHNIQUE PRACTICE
(uchi-komi)

The literal translation of *uchi-komi* is "fitting in (with each other)." In *uchi-komi*, the attacker (*tori*) throws the defender (*uke*), who puts up only a little resistance. Pay attention to proper technique and balance. Do not pick up bad habits in *uchi-komi* because they are hard to change later.

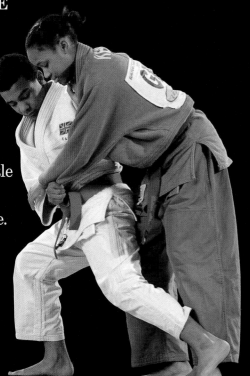

FREE PRACTICE
(randori)

Randori means "catching chaos." It is the judo version of sparring. Partners attack each other as if they are in a competition. *Randori* are usually split into standing *randori* (using throwing techniques) and groundwork *randori* (using hold downs and submissions), but both types of moves can be combined in one *randori* exercise.

Groundwork randori

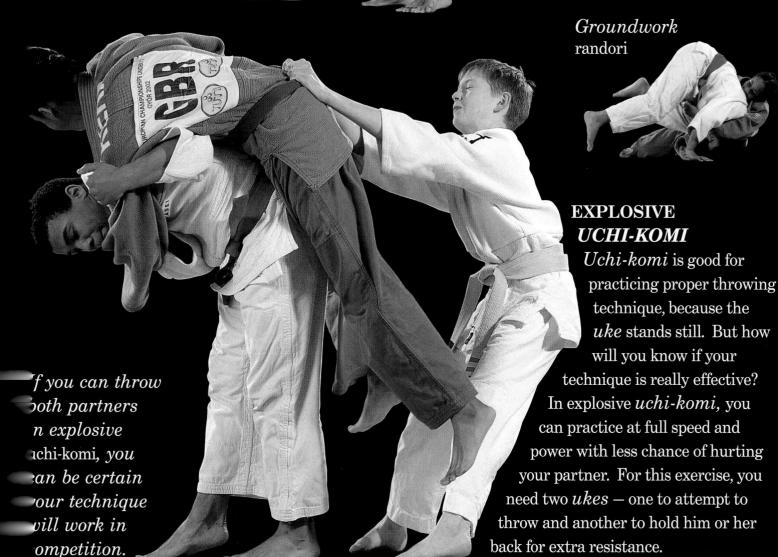

If you can throw both partners in explosive uchi-komi, you can be certain your technique will work in competition.

EXPLOSIVE UCHI-KOMI

Uchi-komi is good for practicing proper throwing technique, because the *uke* stands still. But how will you know if your technique is really effective? In explosive *uchi-komi*, you can practice at full speed and power with less chance of hurting your partner. For this exercise, you need two *ukes* — one to attempt to throw and another to hold him or her back for extra resistance.

HAND TECHNIQUES
(te-waza)

Hand techniques have been developed more than any other judo throwing method. In the first hand techniques, the attacker (*tori*) used only momentum and a twist of the hands to send an opponent to the ground. Many hand techniques required the addition of leg actions to become effective in modern competition. The body drop is one example of this type of hand technique.

BODY DROP *(tai-otoshi)*

1. White takes hold of blue's lapel with his right hand and her sleeve with his left in a conventional right-handed grip.

2. White pulls blue toward him as he steps forward with his right foot, placing it just in front of her right foot.

The floating drop (uki-otoshi) *is the ultimate judo hand technique.*

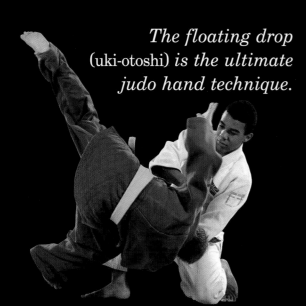

In this body drop, Germany's Udo Quellmalz spreads his legs very wide, but the main move comes from his hands.

3. Turning on the ball of his right foot, white steps around and back with his left foot, then turns his body, facing the same direction blue faces, and pulls blue's sleeve.

4. Blue feels off balance and wants to step forward with her right foot. Before she can, white steps across her right foot, blocking her shin with his calf.

5. White rotates his arms, pushing up with his right and pulling down with his left, and straightens his right knee. Blue falls over his outstretched leg.

EVASION AND COUNTERATTACK WITH INNER THIGH THROW *(uchi-mata)*

1 **2** **3** **4** **5**

1. As white attacks with the body drop, blue starts to move her hips to her right.

2. Blue lifts her right foot and steps over white's throwing leg.

3. Blue places her foot out in front of white as she slips her hips and left leg through.

4. As blue brings her left leg through, she sweeps it inside white's right thigh.

5. Blue pulls hard with her right hand and turns her head and shoulders, throwing white.

OOT SWEEPS
shi-waza)

sweeps are leg throws in which an opponent's foot
g is hooked, swept, or blocked in order to throw him
er. Foot sweeps require speed and good timing.

White hooks blue's leg to pull his feet out from under him.

ANCED FOOT SWEEP *(de-ashi-barai)*

1. White grabs blue with a conventional right-hand grip. He needs to force her to take a step forward so that he can sweep her advancing foot. For this technique to work, white needs to be very loose and relaxed.

2. White takes a step backward with his right foot and pulls blue toward him. This move forces blue to take a step forward with her left foot to regain balance.

EVASION AND COUNTER

The evasion-and-counter moves that work against the advanced foot sweep are both quick and subtle. The defender must dodge the attacker's sweeping foot and catch it with the defender's own advanced foot sweep, all in one swift movement.

1. Blue steps over white's sweeping right foot before it makes contact.

2. Before white can put his foot down, blue catches it with her own foot sweep.

3. Blue sweeps to her right and pulls white down with her left hand.

3

4

3. Just before blue puts her weight on her stepping foot, white quickly steps forward with his right foot, hooking her left ankle with his instep as he lifts her up onto her toes with his hands.

4. White continues to sweep blue's left ankle away to his left as he drags her body down and to his right with his hands. Blue's momentum takes her down to white's right side because she has nowhere to plant her weight.

HIP THROWS
(koshi-waza)

The hips and legs are very powerful weapons in judo. Hip throws, such as the hip wheel (*koshi-guruma*), are often the most spectacular techniques used in a judo match.

In a hip throw, push the hips across the defender's body and use the strength of the legs to launch him or her into the air. Turn your head and shoulders to throw the defender over your hip and onto his or her back.

HIP WHEEL
(koshi-guruma)

1. White holds blue's lapel with her right hand and his sleeve with her left. She creates a small amount of space between herself and blue to move into when she attacks him.

2. White steps between blue's feet and pulls him close by wrapping her arm around his neck. This move secures blue's head and shoulders, giving white control of his torso.

Britain's Michelle Rogers uses a variation on the classic hip throw, spreading her legs and gripping the lapel rather than the sleeve.

BLOCK AND COUNTER

Because the hip wheel is a powerful throw, the evasion and counter must also be powerful.

1. As white turns in with her hip, blue spreads his legs, bends his knees, and sinks his hips lower than white's hips.

2. Gripping tightly around white's waist, blue sits straight down and stretches out his left leg, taking white backward over it in a "valley drop," or *tani-otoshi.*

3. White brings her left foot next to her right, bends her knees, and pulls hard on blue's sleeve as she turns her head and shoulders to the left, bringing blue up onto his toes.

4. White straightens her legs and launches herself forward, rotating her head and shoulders to the left. Blue somersaults and crashes down onto his back.

SACRIFICE THROW
(sutemi-waza)

The sacrifice throw is the riskiest technique in judo because the attacker must fall backward to make the throw.

STOMACH THROW (tomoe-nage)

1   **2**   **3**

1. Because white will throw blue directly over her head, she has a choice of grips. The lapel-sleeve grip she uses is a good choice.

2. White steps in toward blue with her left foot and rolls her fists upward and toward her body to ease blue up onto his toes.

3. White brings her right foot up to blue's abdomen, placing the sole of her foot on the inside of blue's hip, then starts to sit down.

BLOCK AND COUNTER

Blocking the stomach throw is not difficult because the defender can easily slip past the attacking foot or push his or her hips into it to prevent the attacker from straightening the levering leg. To counter the stomach throw, however, the defender must anticipate it.

1. Blue catches white's leg as her foot comes up to his waist.

2. Blue quickly hooks the inside of white's standing leg with a major inner sweep *(o-uchi-gari).*

3. Blue pushes white down to the mat by driving forward with his right hand.

4. White sits down almost on blue's toes. She uses the momentum of her falling body to pull blue down. Keeping her right leg straight and her hands close together, white levers blue off the ground and over her head.

5. White pushes with her foot until blue's momentum takes him over and clear of her body. She keeps a tight grip on his jacket so he cannot twist onto his stomach as he sails through the air and lands on his back.

HOLD DOWNS
(osaekomi-waza)

The simplest way to win a judo contest is by holding down your opponent on his or her back for twenty-five seconds. To win in this way, an attacker must hold a defender's shoulders with a move such as the shoulder hold (*kata-gatame*).

In a hold down, you must secure your partner's shoulders and upper torso. Hold tightly, push your hips down, and spread your legs.

Canada's Aminata Sall uses a variation of kata-gatame, *trapping her opponent's far arm across her face, rather than her near arm.*

SHOULDER HOLD
(kata-gatame)

1

2

3

1. Blue is curled up in the "turtle" position for defense. White gains control over blue by leaning her weight over him.

2. White slips her right arm under blue's right armpit and across his throat. She must do this quickly so he cannot see her arm coming or defend himself against it.

3. White takes hold of her own right hand with her left hand, pulls blue against her chest, and squeezes tightly to prevent him from crawling away.

1

ESCAPE FROM A SHOULDER HOLD

1. Blue turns onto his right hip and reaches over white's body with his left hand to grab onto her belt.

2

2. Blue forces his right hip under white's body as he pulls hard on her belt with his left hand.

3

3. As blue rolls white across his body, he continues pulling on her belt and turns his hips and shoulders to the left.

4. Once white is on her back, blue slips his right arm over white's head and around her neck into a scarf hold (*kesa-gatame*).

4

4   **5**   **6**

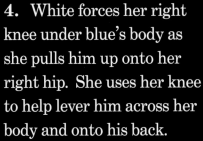

4. White forces her right knee under blue's body as she pulls him up onto her right hip. She uses her knee to help lever him across her body and onto his back.

5. White lies back and rolls blue across her body and onto his back, keeping him on her left-hand side. She uses her momentum to end up on top of blue after the roll.

6. White pushes blue's right arm across his face by leaning her head and shoulder into it. She keeps her weight on her right knee, using her left leg for support.

CHOKES
(shime-waza)

Chokes are one of the two types of submission techniques in judo. They can be applied with the arms, with the legs, or by using the opponent's collar and lapels, as in the sliding collar choke (*okuri-eri-jime*).

The naked choke (hadaka-jime) is a simple and effective choke in which an attacker presses his or her bare wrist against an opponent's windpipe.

SLIDING COLLAR CHOKE
(okuri-eri-jime)

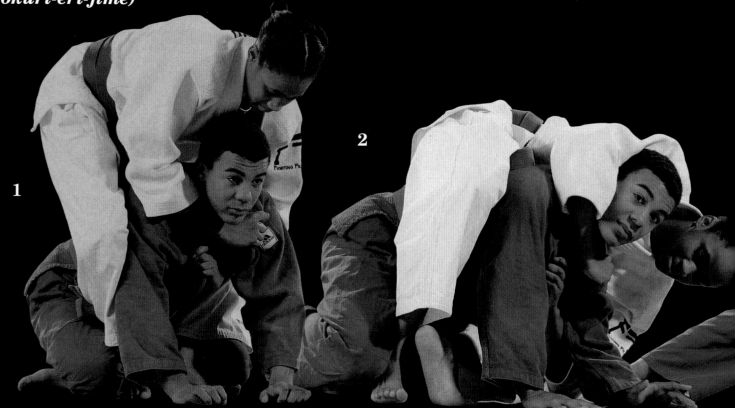

1. Some chokes can begin from in front of an opponent, but the sliding collar choke must be approached from behind. Because blue is defending on all fours, white straddles his back and hooks her legs under his body.

2. With her right hand under blue's chin and her wrist across his throat, white tucks her thumb inside blue's lapel. She then slips her left arm under blue's armpit, grabs his opposite lapel, and begins to roll over.

DEFENSE AGAINST A CHOKE

1. To defend against white's choke, blue must stop white's hand before she gets it up to his throat. If white gets her wrist across his throat, it will be only a matter of time before he submits.

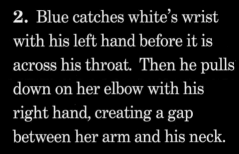

Germany's Udo Quellmalz struggles to apply the sliding collar choke because he has the wrong lapel in his right hand.

2. Blue catches white's wrist with his left hand before it is across his throat. Then he pulls down on her elbow with his right hand, creating a gap between her arm and his neck.

North Korea's Chang Su Li wins against Marc Alexandre of France using a sliding collar choke.

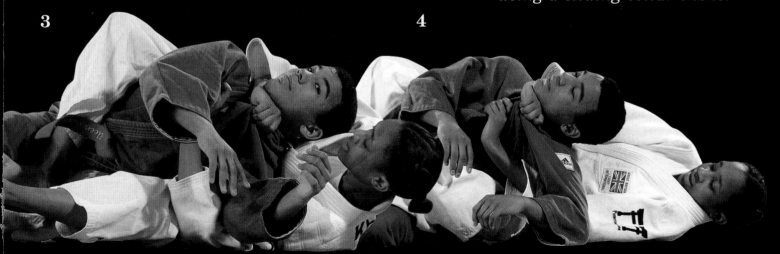

3. As she rolls, white hooks her right foot inside blue's right knee, drives her left leg through the gap under blue's body, and use her left arm to lever his left hand off the mat. Blue will fall onto his left side.

4. White keeps her legs tightly around blue to stretch him out. She pulls his lapel across his throat with her right hand as she pulls down on his opposite lapel with her left hand and tries to straighten her elbows.

ARMLOCKS
(kansetsu-waza)

In an armlock, an attacker pushes an opponent's elbow joint the wrong way. Armlocks can cause a great deal of pain.

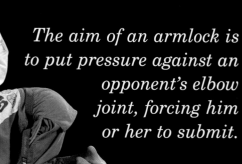

The aim of an armlock is to put pressure against an opponent's elbow joint, forcing him or her to submit.

CROSS ARMLOCK
(juji-gatame)

1. With blue curled up in the turtle position, white climbs on her back and hooks his feet underneath her, reaches across her head with his left hand, and scoops up her right arm.

2. White brings his left knee across the back of blue's neck, to prevent her from moving, rolls onto his shoulder, and grabs her pants leg.

PATTERNS
(kata)

Judo has seven *katas*, or patterns, each of which consists of a series of movements.

Two partners work together to demonstrate their mastery of the techniques of judo in *kata* competitions.

FIRST *KATA*
(nage-no-kata)

The first kata, or *kata* of throws, was designed by Jigoro Kano. It is composed of fifteen throws, grouped into five series of three movements each.

3. Blocking blue's head with his knee, white rolls over his shoulder and onto his back. He heaves blue's legs across his body, rolling her over her own head.

4. With his left leg across her throat and his right leg across her chest, white pulls blue's arm out and pushes his hips against her elbow for the armlock.

Britain's Jamie Johnson uses the cross armlock on a standing opponent.

FOURTH *KATA* (kime-no-kata)

This *kata* uses a variety of locks, strangles, and strikes, sometimes against weapons.

SEVENTH *KATA* (koshiki-no-kata)

This *kata* simulates the battles of Japanese warriors, who fought wearing body armor.

JUDO'S SEVEN *KATAS*

1. *Nage-no-kata* – *kata* of throws
2. *Katame-no-kata* – *kata* on the ground
3. *Gonosen-no-kata* – *kata* of counters
4. *Kime-no-kata* – *kata* of self-defense
5. *Itsutsu-no-kata* – *kata* of the five principles
6. *Ju-no-kata* – *kata* of suppleness
7. *Koshiki-no-kata* – ancient *kata*

USEFUL INFORMATION

If you want to find out more about judo or locate a club near you, the following organizations should be able to help.

Judo Information Site
www.judoinfo.com

United States Judo Association
usja-judo.org

United States Judo Federation
www.usjf.com

USA Judo
www.usjudo.org

All of the Internet addresses (URLs) given in this book were valid at the time of going to press. Due to the dynamic nature of the Internet, however, some addresses may have changed, or sites may have ceased to exist since publication. While the author and publishers regret any inconvenience to readers, they can accept no responsibility for any Internet changes.

Useful addresses:
United States Judo Association
21 N. Union Blvd.
Colorado Springs, CO 80909
(877) 411-3409

United States Judo Federation
P.O. Box 338
Ontario, OR 97914
(541) 889-8753

USA Judo
One Olympic Plaza, Suite 202
Colorado Springs, CO 80909
(719) 866-4730

JUDO TERMS

ashi-waza: foot sweeps

de-ashi-barai: advanced foot sweep

dojo: judo hall

gonosen-no-kata: third kata

hadaka-jime: naked choke

ippon: a knockout score

itsutsu-no-kata: fifth kata

jigotai: defensive posture

judogi: judo uniform

judoka: a person who practices judo

juji-gatame: cross armlock

ju-no-kata: sixth kata

kansetsu-waza: armlocks

kata: patterns

kata-gatame: shoulder hold

katame-no-kata: second kata

kesa-gatame: scarf hold

kime-no-kata: fourth kata

koka: a minor score worth less than a *yuko*

koshiki-no-kata: seventh kata

koshi-guruma: hip wheel

koshi-waza: hip throws

kumi-kata: grip fighting

nage-no-kata: first kata

nage-waza: throwing techniques

obi: judo belt

okuri-eri-jime: sliding collar choke

osaekomi-waza: hold downs

o-uchi-gari: inner sweep

randori: free practice exercises

rei: bow

shime-waza: choking techniques

sutemi-waza: sacrifice throw

tai-otoshi: body drop

tani-otoshi: valley drop

tatami: judo mats

te-waza: hand techniques

tomoe-nage: stomach throw

tori: a competitor who attacks or wins

uchi-komi: technique practice

uchi-mata: inner thigh throw

uke: a competitor who submits or defends

ukemi: breakfalls

uki-goshi: floating hip throw

uki-otoshi: floating drop

waza-ari: a half-point score

yuko: a score worth less than *waza-ari* and more than *koka*

INDEX